A RED DRESS

A RED DRESS
and other poems

Liz Cowley

Illustrations by Dorrance

With a foreword by
Joanna Lumley

CONSTABLE • LONDON

To my daughter, Katy

Constable & Robinson Ltd
3 The Lanchesters
162 Fulham Palace Road
London W6 9ER
www.constablerobinson.com

This edition published by Constable,
an imprint of Constable & Robinson, 2008

A copy of the British Library Cataloguing in Publication
Data is available from the British Library

ISBN: 978-1-84529-854-8

Contents

III
Love & Limits

IV
Love Lost

V
Alone Again

VI
Looking Back

VII
Friends & Enemies

VIII
Autumn Years

Foreword

I was delighted when I first read this collection: delighted by the poignancy, often achieved in a few short words; surprised by the wit and observation that Liz Cowley brings to female experiences and foibles, and touched by the way her poems speak straight to the heart – 'speak' being a particularly apt word. This is 'poetry that talks' as a voice speaks straight from the page, so the effect is like listening rather than reading.

Another thing that interests me is the utter approachability of these poems. So much contemporary poetry can be maddeningly obscure and, at worst, self-indulgent. And, on the other side of the coin, approachable poetry can easily descend into the humdrum or commonplace. Liz strikes that rare balance between being challenging and accessible at the same time, and should move those who never normally like poetry. In fact, I have heard that Liz even dislikes the very word 'poetry' – because she feels there is a divisive ring to it, as if the genre were up there on a rarefied pedestal – and would never dream of describing herself as a 'poet', far preferring the simple 'writer'.

I read this book in a sitting, because I recognized myself in it. I think you will, too – poignant, witty, approachable, straight from the heart.

Joanna Lumley

I

LOVE FOUND

'Relief, he can kiss'

I AM A GROWN-UP

I am a grown-up at last, I say,
I do not need a man to define who I am.
I have long since shed
That insecurity.
I have maturity,
I can be alone –

Until you don't phone.

I am a grown-up at last, I say,
I do not need a man
To be myself and who I am.
I have long since shed
That insecurity,
That need to be a part of two –

Unless the other one is you.

I'M NOT GOING TO GET HURT THIS TIME

I'm careful,
I'm playful,
I'm watchful,
I'm wary.
I'm happy-go-lucky,
I keep the mood airy.

I'm one step behind
All the kindness you show me.
I want you to think
It's not easy to know me.

I'm always dissembling
Whenever you phone me.
I tell you I'm busy
And add, 'You don't own me.'

I say that I'm not free
On Tuesday or Friday,
Though Thursday's a maybe,
But Sunday is my day.

I ask all my girlfriends,

'Did that sound like meanness?'
And want them to tell me,
'It's safer than keenness.'

I'm guarded,
I'm distant,
I'm always pretending.
The truth is
I'm fearful
In case there's an ending ...

And each time I see you
I'm quietly praying
That nothing I'm saying
Is ever betraying
The fact that I've fallen for you.

THE BOOKCASE

The bookcase told her how to date
And find herself a likely mate –
'Are you from Venus or from Mars?
Here's how to read into the stars,
And manage calmly when your mother
Compares you with your married brother.'

The authors told her how it's done
To pull a guy until he's won.
And how to spot a real disaster
Or make the best propose much faster.

The shelves contained three dozen books
On keeping chaps on tenterhooks –
With tips on what they find erotic,
But habits that they think neurotic.
And how to act when on the phone
So they suspect you're not alone.

One night, the bookcase feet away,
I somehow found the strength to say:
'Just be yourself, forget the fools
Who made up all those wretched rules.
You haven't had a man for ages.
No wonder, ploughing through those pages.'

She married Neil in June last year.
I often have them over here.
From their first date, you should have seen them
Without the bookcase in between them.

FIRST TIME

Relief
He's well built.
Relief
He can kiss.
Relief
That he cares,
It's not hit and miss.

Relief
That I like
The taste of his skin.
Relief
That he chose
My bed to be in.

Relief
That he asks
What I like to do,
And chose not to ask,
'And did you come, too?'

IT'S MUCH TOO LATE FOR QUESTIONS

Darling, I must leave you,
It's nearly half past four.
Will you wake up this time
And show me to the door?
Darling, have to go now,
I'm turning on the light,
Wish I didn't have to,
Wish I could stay all night.

Where's the number for the taxi?
Where's my other shoe?
Shall I phone you next time,
Or leave it up to you?

Have to phone now, phone now,
I'm turning on the light,
I'm trying not to wake you,
I'm sorry it's so bright.
Do you love me, love me?
Please say before I go,
Do you love me, love me?
I shouldn't ask, I know.
It's much too late for questions ...

Shall I write a message,
Saying when to call?
Or should I just go quietly,
And tiptoe through the hall?
Shall I make two cups of coffee
To have right now with you?

Or should I leave you sleeping?
Oh, God, what shall I do?

I must leave you, leave you,
Wish I could stay all night.
If I leave you sleeping,
Will you dream of me tonight?
Shall I wake you, wake you,
So you can see me to the door?
Do you love me, love me?
Wish I could feel more sure.
It's much too late for questions ...

Do you love me, love me?
If only you could show
Some sign you really need me
Before I have to go.
Will you phone me, phone me
To make another date?
Can I wake and ask you,
Or is it best to wait?

Where's the number for the taxi?
Where's my other shoe?
Shall I phone you next time,
Or leave it up to you?

THE MAGNOLIA TREE

It's nine o'clock.
I look out of the window at the magnolia tree.
Its blossoms litter the lawn,
Veined and cracked china-white cups spilling death
    on the grass.
Everything is dying around me,
Every day has been grey since you left
And I have not started work on the presentation.

It's ten o'clock.
Fourth cup of coffee.
Startled, I knock it over as the phone rings.
But it's not you.
I sit and stare as a pool spreads slowly
Over the surface of the table
And starts dripping on my dressing gown.

It's eleven o'clock.
I have been watching a bee on the window sill
For five long minutes, struggling, stuck in the sash,
Its buzzing a relief in the deafening silence.
And I am not yet dressed.

It's twelve o'clock
And you phone –
Blessed balm,
Soft, soothing salve,
Calm coolness on a wound.

It's twelve-thirty.
IamraringtogodarlingIloveyouhappy.
The raindrops are diamonds,
The table is gleaming,
The bee has flown free,
The first page of the presentation has written itself
And the magnolia tree will flower again.

THE HAIRDRESSER

'Now how would Madam like her hair?
Let's see, perhaps it's gone too fair.
The colour looks a wee bit dead,
I think it needs a touch of red.

'And how has this month been for you?
I hope that your divorce is through.
I think you mentioned someone new
The last time that I spoke to you?'

'Oh, yes, I'm now a happy ex
And catching up on years of sex.
Well, darling, as I've always said,
Dear Henry was a joke in bed.

'He never once went down on me –
Well, don't you think that's cruelty?
And, God, the man was such a prude –
He loathed me sleeping in the nude.

He used to ask me, "Aren't you cold?"
It made him seem so old, so old.
And then, of course, we had such dramas
When I objected to pyjamas.

Well, now I've found a guy called Dick –
And what a perfect name to pick.
He's so well hung. And what a tongue!
And best of all, he's young! He's young!

With Henry I was half alive,
But Dick is only twenty-five –
And so far doesn't have a clue
I'm coming up to forty-two.

'My, goodness, Madam! What a pair!
And how would Dick prefer your hair?
It's often said young men love red,
You tell me – should I go ahead?'

THE TAXI DRIVER

I do not feel an ounce of shame.
I did not want to know his name,
Or talk to him about his life,
Or ask him if he had a wife.

He, nameless, shameless, just like me,
Fulfilled a simple fantasy.

We hardly spoke a single word,
Or if he did, I barely heard.
And me? Well, I spoke even less –
I only gave him my address.

And three hours later, passion spent,
Anonymous, we came – and went.

I WISH I HAD A SATNAV

I wish I had a Satnav,
A satellite above,
To navigate my journey
Upon the path of love.

'Turn round,' her voice would tell me,
'You're in a cul-de-sac.'
Or 'Straight on, till I warn you,
There is no turning back.'

'Beware!' she would advise me,
'The route is blocked ahead.
And slow down, while you're at it,
The lights are turning red.'

'Slow down!' she would remind me,
'It's time to use the brake!
Too far, too fast,' she'd tell me,
'The commonest mistake.'

'And watch out at the crossroads,
And read the signs with care,
Or else it's twice the effort –
You need to pause right there.'

I've found a lovely fellow
And long to share his life,
But, God, I need a Satnav
If I'm to be his wife.

I'll never make the journey,
I'm sure I'll do things wrong.
I long to have a Satnav –
I've been alone too long.

'You've reached your destination,'
I long to hear her say.
I wish I had a Satnav,
To guide me on my way.

II

LOVE & CONFLICT

'But it didn't show me'

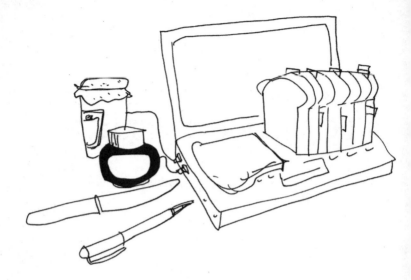

MOTHER OF THE BRAND

We've been in the boardroom since half past three.
I long to be back for my daughter's tea.
I glance at the clock, we're running late,
I will not be home till half past eight.

What do I care about market share
When my daughter cries that I'm not there?
What do I care about Homeblest bread,
Or if the brand is ill or dead?

What do I care about market share
When I would love to brush her hair,
Then see her safely into bed,
And leave my business notes unread?

I long to be giving my daughter tea,
While my daughter longs to remember me.
How could she ever understand?
I am the mother of the brand.

RECIPE

Take a woman and a man –
Sprinkle her liberally with rose petals, blossoms of
    jasmine,
And fine French wine.
(Champagne may also be used.)

To him, add spices, sauce and red-hot pepper.
Whisk constantly.
Blend until smooth; there should be no lumps.
Allow to bubble for two years at maximum heat –
The top should be frothy with golden peaks.

Add a baby, and stir.

Gradually remove all other ingredients, and
Simmer at low temperature for a further two years.

Allow to cool.

Now, take a sharp knife and slice in two.

CUSTODY

Tonight I saw you yet again –
I shouldn't drive that way, it's true –
I saw you at the window pane.
I saw my son, my ex and you.

My son was laughing, so were you,
I had to stop, the lights were red.
I shouldn't take that route, it's true,
That's what all my friends have said.

'He's five,' they say. 'He knows his mother.
He's always with you at weekends.
He knows there can't be any other.'
That's what they all say, my friends.

Accept, that's what I have to do.
You looked so close, the three of you.
For that, I should be happy, too.
My God, if only that were true.

SPORTS DAY

Today is William's sports day,
He thinks he'll win a prize.
I'm going to the office,
I can not meet his eyes.

Today is William's sports day,
I will not see him win.
While he is running, running,
The client's flying in.

Today is William's sports day,
I won't be there. Again.
While he is getting ready,
I'm running for the train.

JOE'S PAINTING

It was lovely, Joe's painting –
'It's the things I like best.'
His playschool art teacher
Was more than impressed.

It was lovely, Joe's painting,
Our house, a huge sun.
And my son was so proud
Of the flowers he'd done.

There was our kitten
And our old apple tree –
'It's the things I like best.'
But it didn't show me.

Yet there was his nanny,
All hands and blonde hair.
Dear Joe, how I wished
That you'd painted me there.

There's a wall in my office
With plenty of space –
I longed for his painting
But not with her face.

THE BIG DEBATE

A survey says that full-time mothers
Are quick to criticize those others
Who, like me, slog at work all day
Because they have to pay their way.

I met one such the other day,
And heard this full-time mother say,
'You work full time? Your child is nine?
I couldn't do the same to mine!'

She carried on, 'It's such a shame,
You give our role a dreadful name.'
I bit my lip, gave scarce a blink
And quickly downed another drink.

But she was quite secure, of course.
She'd quite forgotten that divorce
Can force us out to work all day
And rarely see our children play.

Or else, perhaps, she's none too bright,
And knows that she could earn all right
To cover things she'd like to do –
But not to pay a nanny, too.

Or else – and this may sound unkind –
She may not have the sort of mind
That yearns for challenge, needs to roam,
I have to say, away from home.

Or else, her ex pays handsomely –
A grand a month, or two, or three.
Or else she's married, with a spouse
Who pays the mortgage on the house.

I often wish that full-time mothers
Would pause before attacking others.

III

LOVE & LIMITS

'And you looked at your watch'

THE ROMANTIC

Last week, we went to the sea.
Waves with frothy edges of whipped cream
    dissolving into
Victorian lace and windblown granny curls.
And all underfoot was shining beach jewellery,
Sea-sucked pebbles licked into smooth boiled
    sweets.
The sand was pocked and pimpled by raindrops,
And I wrote our names there –
Sloping,
Slanting,
For the sea to steal and swallow.

And you skimmed a pebble
And said you felt like breakfast.

This week we went to the country.
I looked at fields kissed in mist,
Skybankwater knit in grey wool.
An army of shining blades glittered at our feet.
Gossamer sacs cradled dewdrops.
I looked at spiked conker cases littering the path
Robbed of their inmates by laughing children,
At russet rotting apples lying on lawns,
Mildew fluffed fruit oozing juice,
At naked trees sighing and leaves flying.

And you looked at your watch.

MAPS

My husband is the gentle type,
Except when in a car –
He thinks we women never know
Exactly where we are.

He thinks we choose a tree or pub
To plot the road ahead,
And never knowing north from south,
Go east or west instead.

In fact, he thinks we're spatial fools
Who can not read a map –
Though even when I know my way
He slaps one on my lap.

'Now keep it there!' he barks at me,
'Don't hide the thing away!'
'But, darling heart, I worked right here,
And drove past every day!'

He thinks we can not read a map
(Or read it upside down)
And every time I say, 'Next right',
He speeds on with a frown.

And when I say, 'But, darling heart,
You've gone one turn too far,'
He says that he will read the map,
And I must drive the car.

My husband's like a lot of chaps
Whenever in a car –
He thinks that women never know
Exactly where we are.

CHRISTMAS

I've wrapped all the gifts,
I've put up the tree,
I've hung up the cards –
He's on the first tee.

I've made the mince pies,
I've done the bread sauce –
He's off playing golf,
It's par for the course.

I've mended the lights,
I've basted the duck –
He's now in a bunker
Bemoaning his luck.

I've worked out the table,
We're having fourteen.
I've polished the silver –
Now he's on the green.

I've hung up the wreath,
It's on the front door –
He's on the sixteenth,
He'll do it in four.

At six, he'll be back,
Poor over-tired soul,
And I'll have to listen
To hole after hole.

I'll smile when he says,
'The day was quite fun.'
But not when he asks,
'And what have *you* done?'

RESIGNATION

I'm honest – I admit I'm fat.
I'm truthful – I'll admit to that.
I'm sick and tired of calories
Or what the newest diet is,
And all those boring magazines,
With skinny models in their jeans.

I'm honest – I admit the truth.
I've put on five stone since my youth.
I like to eat sweet things like cake –
The kind my mother used to make.

Ah, that's my husband coming in,
He's quite the opposite – he's thin.
He hates to see me eat like this:
You'll see, I never get a kiss.

He hates the way I go to bed
At nine o'clock and overfed.
I'm always fast asleep by ten –
We never will have sex again.
The last time? Oh, good heavens alive,
It must be nineteen eighty-five.

He takes his girlfriend to his club.
He met her at the local pub.
She's slim – that's what appeals to him.
She works down at the local gym.

Oh, yes, he knows. He knows I know.
But somehow, I don't think he'll go.
The choice is simple: me and fat,
Or moving to a poky flat.

And now – I'd like a slice of cake.
Don't *stare* at me for heaven's sake!

MOUSE

He is married to his job
And I am married to our house.
He trapped a tiger years ago
And turned her into me, a mouse.

While I buy carpets, he buys shares
To leave to all his sons and heirs.
I do not care when he's not there,
We never do things as a pair.

We both know that we'll never split.
We'd hate the heavy price of it.
And so we share the marriage bed
Long after all desire is dead.

The house is always spick and span,
I have a maid and handy man.
I'm quite content to live this way –
Well, just as long as he can pay.

He is married to his job
And I am married to our house.
He trapped a tiger years ago
And turned her into me, a mouse.

The will to roam has long since gone,
I'm too old to be moving on.
I'm living in a money cage –
There could be worse things at my age.

SWITCHING OFF

So many things I used to love are now an irritation –
The way you use such complex words to spice your
    conversation,
The way you always interrupt when someone else is
    talking,
And never ever make the bed, and lag behind when
    walking.

So many things I used to love now fill me with
    frustration –
The way you phone me every night to say you're at
    the station,
Or, when you're back from business trips to
    Düsseldorf or Galway,
The way you check the answerphone no sooner
    through the hallway.

So many things I used to love now drive me to a
    fury –
The way that you pontificate as if you're judge and
    jury,
And always lift my saucepan lids to check my stews
    and sauces,
Then ask me if that's all there is, and what the
    second course is.

So many things I used to love, but now hate with a
    passion –
Your clothes, the way you wear your hair, your
    ghastly sense of fashion.
All love has gone, I must move on – so much that
    drives me crazy.
I would have left you years ago, if I were not so lazy.

OUCH

I'm a man's kind of woman,
All menfolk love me:
The secret is simple –
I listen, you see.

If they air opinions,
I never compete,
And all men adore it,
It works like a treat.

I tell them they're clever
And charming and wise,
Or else I just listen
And stare with big eyes.

I keep out of things
Like Iraq and the war,
And business and death
And what we're here for.

Men don't want a woman
Who acts like a man,
While wearing the trousers
Whenever she can.

I'm always in dresses
And shoes with a heel,
Five or six inches,
However they feel.

I'm a man's kind of woman,
Men say that of me:
Whatever they think,
I don't disagree.

I've no time for women,
They're jealous you see –
They all know their husbands
Would far prefer me.

WHEN THERE'S A WILL

'Remember summers at the sea,
Just Mum and Dad, and you and me?
Remember cricket on the beach?
The ball kept flying out of reach.

'Remember that old apple tree?
Mum loved our tree house, didn't she?
Remember that fantastic cake,
The chocolate one she used to bake?

'Remember once when you were seven,
You asked her, "What's it like in heaven?"
She said, "Well, that is far away,
But all of us will die, one day." '

'Shut up. They're complex, their affairs.
There's fifty grand in stocks and shares
And twenty necklaces and rings –
My wife has asked for certain things.

'And then, I see, there's quite a stash
Of twenty grand in ready cash.
And plenty of fine silver, too,
That comes to me, and not to you.

'It all goes to the only son,
As that is how it's always done.
I also get the antique chest
Because it has the family crest.'

'Remember summers at the sea,
Just Mum and Dad and you and me?'

MOBILES

Oh, yes, the meeting turned out fine.
Expect me back at half past nine.
Before I am, though, one small task,
A favour that I'd like to ask –
Please, could you put the washing in?
It's mostly in the laundry bin,
No, actually, there is some more –
Of course, it's on the bedroom floor.
And, darling, don't forget my tights.
I think they're hanging on the lights,
Or else they're on the bedside table.
I'm sure that even you are able
To put them in at number three.
That would be such a help to me!
Hang on, don't put the knickers in –
I know the gusset's wearing thin.
I think the label says, 'By hand'.
What, darling, don't you understand?
A gusset? That's the middle bit.
Oh, darling, you are such a twit!
No, darling! Do I have to shout?
I said to leave the knickers out!

IV

LOVE LOST

'I think we need a breathing space'

THE VASE

After an affair
Everyone is so keen to help you
Sweep away the pieces –
Like shards of shattered glass
Too dangerous to tread.

I wish they would put away the brushes.
I want to keep the pieces so I can puzzle out the
     pattern
And the break.

I want to gather up the fragments that remain,
That nothing be lost.

That way, I'll make a beautiful vase next time
For someone to fill with flowers.

A BREATHING SPACE

'I think we need a breathing space.'
She means, I'm tiring of your face.

'I need some quiet time alone.'
She means, don't try to text or phone.

'I feel I am not right for you.'
She means, the opposite is true.

'The fact is, you're too good for me.'
She means, it's over, can't you see?

'I'm thinking of the two of us.'
She means, let's split without the fuss.

'I'm just confused, I can't explain.'
She means, to do so is a strain.

'Right now, I've so much on my mind.'
She means, I hope I'm sounding kind.

'I don't know what I want in life.'
She means, it's not to be your wife.

'You've always been so very kind.'
She means, I want a sharper mind.

'My ex is still there in my head.'
She means, he was more fun in bed.

'I've never met a man like you.'
She means, I'm ripe for someone new.

'I half suspect you feel the same.'
She means, you're more than half to blame.

'Perhaps it's just too much, too fast.'
She means, the golden times are past.

'We can not simply carry on.'
She means, because the spark has gone.

'I'll always love you, that's for sure.'
She means, I'm showing you the door.

'We'll always be the best of friends.'
She means, goodbye, that's where it ends.

A RED DRESS

They were on the balcony below —
Ten feet and a thousand miles apart from us.
I heard them at night, while you were sleeping.

They read each other
While you read *The Decline and Fall of the Roman
    Empire*
And I read road maps
And worked out where to go for lunch.

One day I slipped out at dawn
And walked three miles along the beach
Without telling you I was leaving.
You came after me, hot and cross —
You were ten feet and a thousand miles apart from me
When I first saw you clearly.

I bought a red dress
To wear on our last night.
But you didn't notice it
Until I asked what you thought
And you asked what it cost.

Our marriage.
I wore a red dress to a funeral.

BUSES

I knew there was no hope for us
The day you said, 'Let's go by bus.'

Love's journey does not go with stopping
And staring out at people shopping,
Or watching them climb off and on.
Before Earl's Court, desire had gone.

How lust is crushed by commonsense
And thinking of the pounds and pence:
'It's madness to take up the car,
You know how pricey car parks are.'

We saved a packet, that is true,
It only cost a quid or two –
But isn't thrift a wee bit silly
If love stops short of Piccadilly?

What less romantic thing to do
Than watch out for the 22,
While standing in a rain-soaked queue
With losers piled ahead of you?

Who wants to hear that tuneless chugging
And watch exhausted mothers lugging
Their wretched baby buggies on?
By Fulham, all romance had gone.

It left the bus that very day,
When South Ken was four stops away.

THE LAST MOMENT

One chance remark,
One hint,
One word
You can't pretend you haven't heard;
One comment,
Just one glance,
One look
Can mark the last page in a book.

No matter, two years,
Three years, more,
That one remark can slam a door.
You see or hear a different man
You never came across before.

I didn't want to hear or see,
But now I have, you're dead for me.
Too late to ask you to explain.
There is no going back again.

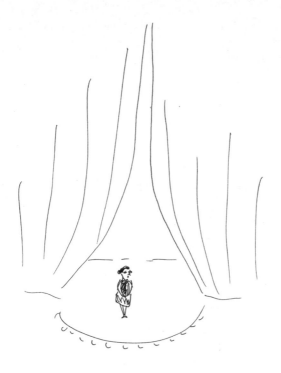

THE WINGS

Ever since you left, I have been sitting in the wings,
Watching the play in silence, while others laugh,
And studying the women centre stage, drawing the
    spotlight
With the witty lines I have forgotten.
I am alone, on the wrong side of the curtain.
The cast can not see me in the darkness,
And I do not want to be up there
Acting.

THE WEDDING

'Amazing wedding! All those flowers!'
'And Krug and caviar for hours!'
'And what a castle! What a lake!
All floodlit, too, for heaven's sake!'

'And what a crowd – in three marquees!'
'Plus ice-cream parlour, if you please!'
'And what a ball! And what a band!
It must have cost a hundred grand!'

'And what a super springy floor!
That must have cost four thousand more!'
'And what a gift for every guest!
Bulgari, Asprey, and the rest!'

'And what a dress! And what a ring!
And, wow, Oasis there to sing!'
'And what a car! And what a plane
To fly them – privately – to Spain!'

'And what a shame they split so fast!
When was the wedding? Tuesday last?'

OVERHEARD

'Are you with her tonight?' she said.
I knew the way her question led.
I listened to how you replied,
And knew just what your words implied.

You didn't know that I could hear,
That I was just a step away.
In fact, it came through loud and clear,
That you and I were yesterday.

'Are you with her tonight?' she said.
'*Tonight*, I am,' I heard you say.
I heard you kill a marriage dead,
Just three words blew it all away.

V

ALONE AGAIN

'I had everything I needed – except you'

SINGLE TICKETS

'I rather fancy Vietnam.
Or this looks interesting – Guam.'
'And so does this, the Ile de Ré.'
'Oh, darling, France? That's so passé.'

'Or here looks nice. It's Rajasthan.
Or this, it's somewhere in Japan.'

'Do Ryanair do cheap flights there?
We haven't all got cash to spare.'

'Girls, how about a nice safari,
Or camping in the Kalahari?'

'We'd boil to death in south Botswana –
Here, take a look at trips to Ghana.
A load of chaps who'd like you there –
They'd love the fact you have blonde hair.
And, better still, since your divorce,
You've heaps to spend on them of course.'

'Could someone tell me – where is Guam?
Oh, ignoramus that I am!
Ah, yes, it says the west Pacific.
The food might not be that terrific.'

'Oh, darling, please don't call it "Gwam",
Like ham and spam and raspberry jam.
It rhymes with palm and inner calm,
Or think of your new Porsche alarm.'

'I know, let's go to east Croatia,
Or riding right through Central Asia!
Of course, we'd need a jab or two,
Well, don't the birds give people flu?'

'*You*? You'd never last the course.
I can't see you upon a horse.
And, anyway, I don't like slumming,
Or anywhere without good plumbing.'

'I'd far prefer a bit of life.
We're all divorced, not someone's wife.
A place in Spain, with lots of clubs.
And blokes. And English in the pubs.'

'Oh, Alice, dear, you're fifty-two.
The locals wouldn't glance at you!
You could, of course, choose Mexico
And hitch up with a gigolo.'

'Well, thanks, and count me out this year.
And tell me, girls, what's wrong with here?
Why must we always go abroad?'
'That's clear, my dear. We're bored. We're *bored*.'

COSTA BRAVA

With skin near skin
And Spanish gin
And days to laze
Beneath the haze,
We fast forget a golden rule;
It's easy to become a fool
Around a palm-fringed swimming pool.

With sun-bleached hair
In splendid tangles
And bodies at exciting angles,
What do you do?
What do you do?
I don't write postcards home, do you?

They vanish, all the 'ifs' and 'buts'
When liquid oils of coconuts
Are smoothed on limbs, now silky sleek.
We say, 'I'm here for just a week.'

No wonder, boosted by a tan
We find a quite appalling man –
The best, maybe, in our hotel,
But back at home, right out of hell.

THE SPLIT

I flew abroad for a fortnight
And told you to take everything you thought was
    yours.
And leave the rest.
I thought it best.

You were fair,
As I knew you would be.
You were fair,
As you knew you should be.

Everything I needed was still there
When I returned.
In fact, you more than passed the test.
You left the best,
Like the mirror and the chair
We bought on our tenth anniversary.

I had enough
Knives and forks
And dishes
And glasses
And pictures
And books.

I had everything I needed –
Except you.

PLASTIC SURGERY

When I had plastic surgery
I went right back to thirty-three.
And now I'm with much younger men,
But wish I could change back again.

The problem? Though I like their waists,
I can not stand their awful tastes.
Who wants to sit through endless sport
Or talk of what was missed or caught?

And who can bear the sound of rap,
However handsome any chap?
And who can take eight hours of sex,
While crushed beneath two steamy pecs?

Who wants to jive till half past five
Then crawl home only half alive?
And who wants so much time alone?
While they're at work, I'm on my own.

Worse, who wants all that beery pubbing –
Or constant dreary evenings clubbing?
I've done that sort of thing before
And now I find it all a bore.

But now the nicest older guys
Don't fancy me. They think it's wise
To pick a woman of their age,
Not someone at a different stage.

Outside, I'm only thirty-three –
They don't see the inside of me.
And, then, when they have seen my face,
They think they can't keep up the pace.

I wish I could go back to me
Before the plastic surgery.
Misjudgement is my second name.
I've only got myself to blame.

BLUNDER

'*Doesn't* my old man dress well?
He always looks so good in blue!
Doesn't my old man dress well?
That suit and shirt and tie are new!
Doesn't my old man dress well?
You'd never guess he's fifty-two!
Doesn't my old man dress well?'

'Oh, yes. And very quickly, too.'

WOMAN TO WOMAN

'You can't know till you try it!'
'Oh, yes, I'm sure that's true.'

'At least you don't deny it,
A lot of women do.'

'Oh, no, I don't deny it.
It's just I'm happy straight –
I've never once been tempted.'
'Well, now is not too late.'

'I think it is, my darling,
I'm nearly thirty-three.
If I were gay, I'd know it.'
'That's often said to me.'

'I'm sorry, but it's midnight.
I've got a heavy day.'

'Then why not use the spare room?
Relax – I'll keep away.
But still – you ought to try it,
Or else you'll never know.'

'I'm sure, I won't deny it,
But now I need to go.'

VI

LOOKING BACK
'It sounds like quite another life'

THE PLAY

I see you, you do not see me,
I'm right behind you in row C.
I watch you, as you watch the play,
I'm deaf to what the actors say.

I used to love your cloud of hair,
So thick, so wild in wind, corn fair.
But now your scalp is shiny red
And sweat beads glisten on your head.

Your collar is too tight on you,
A larger size is overdue.
You're bald. Seem shorter. Overweight.
And flustered from arriving late.

Is that your wife with sprigs of grey?
I guess I have a few today.
If we meet later, what to say?
How much we both enjoyed the play?

You drop the programme on the floor
And find retrieving it a chore.
Your waistband stops you reaching down.
You shuffle, fidget, scratch and frown.

Can it be true? Can it be true?
The man in front of me is you?
I marvel now at all the tears
That ended almost twenty years.

You whisper something to your wife.
I'm glad I have another life.

The curtains open for Act Two
And close at last on me and you.

THE LIAR

You lied when you talked about college,
You fibbed when you talked about school.
Your knowledge of flying is sketchy,
I was never that much of a fool.

At Cresta, they don't seem to know you.
The Ferrari you had was not yours.
I knew you did not go to Davos,
I was never that blind to your flaws.

I knew you had not been to Cambridge.
I knew you had not got a first.
Of all your huge lies, and vast porky pies,
Those surely must score as your worst.

I knew you had not been to Egypt,
Your knowledge of ancients was weak.
I knew you had not skied in Aspen,
Knew it all from the very first week.

So why did I bother to date you?
Quite simple – you're marvellous in bed.
Who cares that you talked about Tolstoy
And authors I knew you'd not read?

By Christmas, you started to bore me.
And that was just seventeen days.
If you hadn't talked, I wouldn't have walked,
We'd have tried it a dozen more ways.

But how do you tell a good lover,
'You're a drag when you get out of bed?'
I found a way how, and that's why I'm now
Quite happily single instead.

16
My bedroom is a shrine to me,
A photographic library.
Every photo that you see
Is luscious, gorgeous, pretty me.

26
Today it is a sanctuary.
I have some photos, two or three,
But only of my chap and me,
The two of us, it's love you see.
I've stored the other ones away,
I'll look at them again some day.

36
I keep two photos in the place
I sit to do my hair and face –
My daughter, snapped at one and three,
There's not a single one of me.

46
Those same two photographs are there
While she has dozens everywhere,
And always her at centre stage,
Well, just like I was at her age.

56
And now it's almost ten years on,
And, sadly, Mum and Dad have gone.
I keep a photo by my bed,
One taken on the day they wed.

66

The photographs are changing places,
And now I have two other faces –
Two grandsons smiling out at me,
One six years old, the other three.

The wedding one's been taken out.
Well, Alexander's not about.
I rather liked my son-in-law,
But we won't see him any more.

76

Today, we're mostly on our own,
My photo collection, though, has grown.
I have another face around,
Dear Belle, our faithful Basset Hound.

And when I comb my thinning hair,
I like another photo there,
Of us, our ruby wedding day.
I've tucked the other ones away.

86

Downstairs there's hardly any space
To try and fit another face.
But upstairs now there's one of me,
A photograph at twenty-three,
All smiles and freshness, flowing hair.
I thought it best to move it there.

Last time my grandsons came to call
They stopped below it in the hall,
And one of them, if not the two,
Said, 'Grandma, is that *really* you?'

DIVORCE

'See that house up on the hill?
If you look hard, you'll see her still –
My ghost upon the window sill.'

Her son looks up
Sees nothing there,
A pause hangs on the summer air.
Memories floating on the breeze
Suffuse her as if some disease.

A minute passes,
Then, a sigh –
'You're not a ghost.
You didn't die!'

'A little bit,' he hears her say.
'I'll tell you how, another day.'

MY EX FRED

My ex Fred was a dreary old soul,
A dreary old soul was he –
An old-fashioned type who smoked on his pipe
And was sixty by forty-three.

My ex Fred was a boring old soul,
A City accountant he,
And night after night, he kept on the light,
While he read through the whole *FT*.

My ex Fred was a sleepy old soul,
A snorer in front of TV –
And it has to be said, a dullard in bed,
Who never did much for me.

My ex Fred was a thoughtless old soul,
A thoughtless old soul was he –
Now twenty years on, he's noticed I've gone,
And friends say he's missing me.

'Jim Wilson had the finest mind
And, best of all, was truly kind.
Our feelings go to Jane, his wife,
And all those here who shared his life.
Jim was generous, warm and witty
And so successful in the City.
What's more, a legend it is said
When on the board of RTZ,
As such a sympathetic boss
If anybody made a loss.
Jim was caring. Jim was funny.
Jim dedicated all his money
To helping people out in life.
Our feelings go to Jane, his wife.'

'Psst! Is this funeral for Jim?
It doesn't sound a bit like him!
And I should know – I'm Jane, his wife.
It sounds like quite another life.'

VII

FRIENDS & ENEMIES

'A shoulder to cry on'

FOF

FOF, Fear of Failure, do you know FOF?
Boy, if you do, you won't pull it off.
Always behind you, as if he's your friend.
Always beside you, and right to the end.

If you want to sing, then why sing that song?
FOF will assure you, you're getting it wrong.
FOF is all powerful, stronger than you,
Constantly telling you what you *can't* do.

You want to act? He'll be at your shoulder –
'Please give it up before you're much older.
Ninety per cent of you end up as waiters,
Or, if you're lucky, become second-raters.'

FOF, Fear of Failure, do you know FOF?
Try as you might, you can't shake him off.
Always behind you, as if he's your friend.
Always beside you, and right to the end.

He'll tell you it's simpler just not to try.
He'll never, I promise, bid you goodbye.
Whatever you do, he'll tell you it's wrong,
The book or the poem, the play or the song.

He's a wit, he's a cynic, he's often amusing.
With FOF, all succeeding is second to losing.
He'll tell you it's simpler just not to try,
And so, in the end, your talents just die.

FOF is all powerful, stronger than you,
Always reminding you what you can't do.
FOF, Fear of Failure, do you know FOF?
Boy, if you do, friend, you won't pull it off.

FAIR-WEATHER ENEMY

She's a great friend, is Sheila.
Well, great in disaster –
She couldn't come faster
If everything's doom.
She's my anchor in trouble,
But off at the double
If I've found a new partner
And all is not gloom.

She's a great friend, is Sheila.
She's not a scene-stealer –
I've known her for years
And years with no man.
She couldn't come faster
If there's a disaster,
But if life's all rosy,
Then she never can.

She's a great friend, is Sheila.
A shoulder to cry on –
The one I rely on
At times of despair.

But, if I'm contented
Then she goes demented.
I'd love to ask why
But I never quite dare.

She's a great friend, is Sheila.
She'd like my new partner –
But won't come around
To meet him and see.
I can cry on her shoulder
As I've always told her,
But if it's all laughter
She never sees me.

MAGAZINES

Another ten facelifts –
'TIME FOR THE KNIFE?
READ HOW THESE WOMEN
SLICED YEARS OFF THEIR LIFE!'

Another confession,
Another 'New Star'
(They always assume
You know just who they are).

Another dull column
On 'Finding Yourself',
And self-help disasters,
'Must-haves' for your shelf.

Another top actress
Embroiled in divorce,
Expecting a pay-off
Of millions, of course.

Another two-pager
On 'This season's bags',
And what's on the arm
Of celebrity WAGs.

Another free pull-out –
TOP-20 HEALTH CHECKS,
And, yes, a huge survey
On 'Fabulous Sex!'

Another six pages,
'MEET JORDAN AT HOME!
Your chance to explore
Her palazzo in Rome!'

Another old chestnut
On Hollywood teens –
Hello! No! Goodbye
To all magazines.

DINNER PARTIES

Now, how about a main of fish
And that great sauce I did with lime?
Oh, blast, I'm sure that was the dish
I gave to John and Sue last time.

A boeuf en croûte? I do that well,
It's always something of a treat.
Oh, damn and blast and bloody hell,
Suzanne and Philip don't eat meat.

Paella? That might fit the bill –
I got quite good at that in Spain.
No, hang on, prawns make Anna ill,
She says they give her stomach pain.

I know, I'll do a salmon trout.
Oh, no! Diana always moans,
Unless the backbone's taken out,
And all those fiddly little bones.

Or why not take the whole lot out?
No, that idea is truly daft.
They'll all assume the meal's my shout
And double up my overdraft.

Oh, damn and hell, a day to go,
And still I'm stuck for what to do.
There *must* be something. Ah, I know!
I'll ring and say I've just caught flu.

SEX COLUMNS

I wish that sex were half as good
As magazines all say it is.
There must be something wrong with me
If that's the truth, the way it is.

The G-spot? Is it fact or myth?
I've searched the damned thing everywhere.
Perhaps some chap invented it?
Well, can you find it anywhere?

They tell me that I can achieve
Ten climaxes in quick succession.
But that I truly can't believe,
I'm lucky with just one a session.

And what about the afterglow
Some females seem to have for hours?
You lucky girls, I've come to know
Such glowing is beyond my powers.

They tell me, change your operandi
And venture out upon a mission
(While keeping a vibrator handy)
To change a habit; one position.

My chap on top is fine for me –
Perhaps I'm dull not wanting more.
And, frankly, I like sex in bed
And not upon the kitchen floor.

I often wonder if it's me
Who's simply somewhat un-erotic,
Or whether reading magazines
Is what is making me neurotic?

THE PHONE CALL

'Today it's my yoga, and cricket for Tim,
And then driving Flora to Twickenham gym,
And on to my art course, starting at two –
The whole day is hectic, so much to do.

'Monday's the school run, and then it's my hair.
I have to look nice, with Edward as Chair.
We're out the same evening, so that's busy too.
We're off around six to a big business do.

'Tuesday is useless. All morning, it's bridge,
And then it's to Waitrose to fill up the fridge,
And afterwards, tennis, starting at three,
Then Flora is having her whole class to tea.

'The evening? Forget it. They won't leave till five,
And I'd be a wreck by the time you arrive.
Plus one of the parents can't get here till nine,
The sort who expects at least one glass of wine.

'No, Wednesday's no good – it's Flora's school play,
And making her costume will take me all day.
Then Thursday's the day we clear up the stage
And take back the props. It all takes an age.

'On Friday, of course, is my cookery class,
And drinks in the evening. How the days pass!
I'm sorry, my darling, but I have to fly.
The week is quite frantic. Must say goodbye.'

LOST

I knew at once that I wanted you.
I loved your full mouth,
Your smooth skin,
Your surprises,
Your inner strength.

Holding you was security in an uncertain world.
You made sense of the muddle
And my secrets were safe within your heart.

But now I have lost you
And my life is in limbo.
I am condemned to wander aimlessly
From room to room,
Paralysed, unable to go out,
Aching for the touch and feel of you,
And picturing you on someone else's arm.

My life,
My core,
My anchor,
My very existence,
My handbag – where are you?

VIII

AUTUMN YEARS

'Season of new-found sisterhood'

INVISIBLE

At twenty, I could turn a head
Whenever walking down the street.
In fact, I turned a dozen heads.
It's true, I promise, not conceit.

At thirty, walking down the street
I turned a head, or two, or three.
And workmen often downed their tools
To take a closer look at me.

At forty, walking down the street
Some turned their heads, but turned away.
They rarely eyed me up and down,
And just continued on their way.

At fifty, walking down the street
They never saw me pass at all.
They simply walked and stared ahead,
Expressions blank, just like a wall.

And now I'm sixty-five years old
And, once again, they stare at me.
The whole world looks me up and down –
My leg is plastered up, you see.

I broke it falling down the stairs,
A rather silly thing to do.
The unexpected bonus is
I'm absolutely back on view.

The whole street looks me up and down
From toe to top, and top to toe.
It's lovely to be seen again.
It's splendid to be back on show.

SEVENTIES

Less years ahead than the ones left behind.
More and more specs, as without them you're blind.
Less and less done, since you're always too tired.
Less and less work – well, at sixty you're fired.

More and more time, now the children have flown.
Less and less visits – they all use the phone.
Less and less hair, and more and more grey.
More and more wrinkles that won't go away.

More and more times you hear yourself say,
'We didn't do things like that in our day.'
Less and less programmes you like on TV.
Less and less people you're burning to see.

More and more time spent travelling abroad.
More and more money spent getting insured.
Less and less healthy, and more and more tweaks,
And more and more aches that won't go for weeks.

More and more thoughts that go through your head
Of friends who have gone, and things left unsaid.
More and more times when you sit down and think,
How could I manage without a stiff drink?

AUTUMN YEARS
(apologies to John Keats and 'To Autumn')

Season of depth, new-found contentedness,
Close bosom friend of many women now,
Conspiring with them how to worry less
About the tiny crow's feet on the brow,
And how to fill the days with merry laughter,
And fill more nights with friends around to sup,
And care much less about the morning after,
And wait till then to do the washing up.
Season of calm, and new-found sisterhood,
No enemy of any woman now,
No lies, betrayals, no conspiracies,
No other woman hissing, 'Bloody cow'.

'WHAT DO YOU MOST LIKE
IN BED?'

'What do you most like in bed?'
At twenty, I was somewhat shy.
'Oh, just the usual things,' I said,
Or let the question pass me by.

'What do you most like in bed?'
By twenty-eight, I told them straight,
Unless I thought I was in love,
In which case I would hesitate.

'What do you most like in bed?'
At forty-five, I said, 'Just you,'
While somewhat miffed that I was asked
By now, I hoped my husband knew.

'What do you most like in bed?'
He hasn't asked me that of late.
Well, he is almost sixty-five,
And I'm just short of fifty-eight.

Thank God the old chap knows at last
Exactly what I find sheer heaven –
A cracking book I haven't read
And coffee brought at half past seven.

WELL, WELL, WELL

'Hi! You're looking really well!'
A greeting that I've come to hate.
The day they say you're looking well,
You know you're past your sell-by date.

THE THIRTEEN AGES
OF WOMAN
(apologies to William Shakespeare and
'The Seven Ages of Man')

All the world's a stage,
And all the girls and women merely players –
We have our exits and our entrances,
And females in our time play many parts,
Our acts now thirteen ages.

At first, the infant,
Mewling and puking in our au pair's arms.

Then, the whining schoolgirl, with our lunchbox
And grumpy morning face, creeping like snail
Unwillingly to school.

And next the girlfriend,
Texting like crazy
With a woeful message sent to our boyfriend's
    BlackBerry.

Then the student, full of strange drinks,
Horrendous while at home, jealous in friendship,
Sudden and quick in quarrel, seeking a drunken
    adulation,
Mostly in the Uni bar.

And then the worker, clubbing till cock-crow,
Now with pockets lined, and eyes bloodshot
From staying out, again,
Full of remorse while getting on the train.
And so we fluff our job.

Next act, the lover, on passion's mountain climb
Of peaks and troughs,
Through countless falls
Until the primrose path that lies beyond.

And now the mother, in fair round belly
With our firstborn lined,
Our eyes dew soft, our skin in springtime bloom,
Full of wise saws on what to do,
Playing centre stage.

The eighth age shifts
Into the sleek and envied mother–wife,
With youthful waist well kept and thighs gym
        slim,
With self-tanned glow, and sweet maternal voice
Turning again towards childish treble,
Strange coos and coaxes in our sound.

Scene nine now starts to mar this strange eventful
        history
As passion exits stage. Divorcée, spitting,
Splitting up the spoils of house and home
And hapless family. A tiny flat now beckons,
Plus a job. Love lost and labour gained
In one fell swoop, the end of salad days.

Now enters stage
The older second spouse.
A tough act this, we act as best we can
While crying that our children spoil the scene
Because they loathe the lead, the second man.

Those dramas gone,
Our offspring join the cast,
Invited to the thatchèd country home
Through rosebud porch, our secateurs at hand,
Our Aga roasting and a wine glass poured,
With Sunday lunch neat laid upon the stage.

The twelfth age moves
Into the silver stages of our play,
With travel to the globe's exotic places,
The mortgage bills by now a world away.

Last scene, thirteen,
That crowns our role, our rollercoaster life,
Grandmother, mother, friend, contented wife,
Exulting in the part that's yet to come,
Now ripe and ready for a final fling –
With teeth, with eyes, with cash, with everything.

Index of titles and first lines